# A Trip to the Doctor

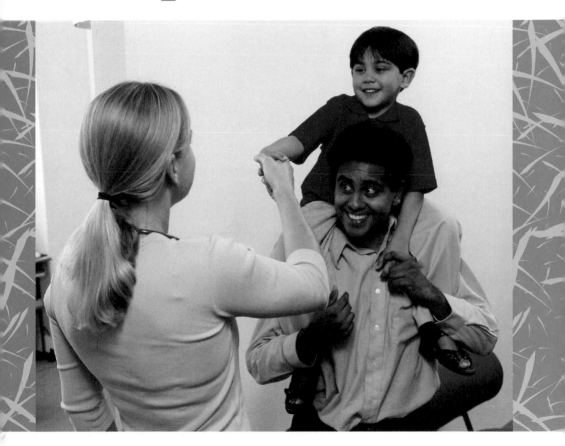

## Jan Pritchett

# My doctor takes care of me.

# My doctor takes care of me.

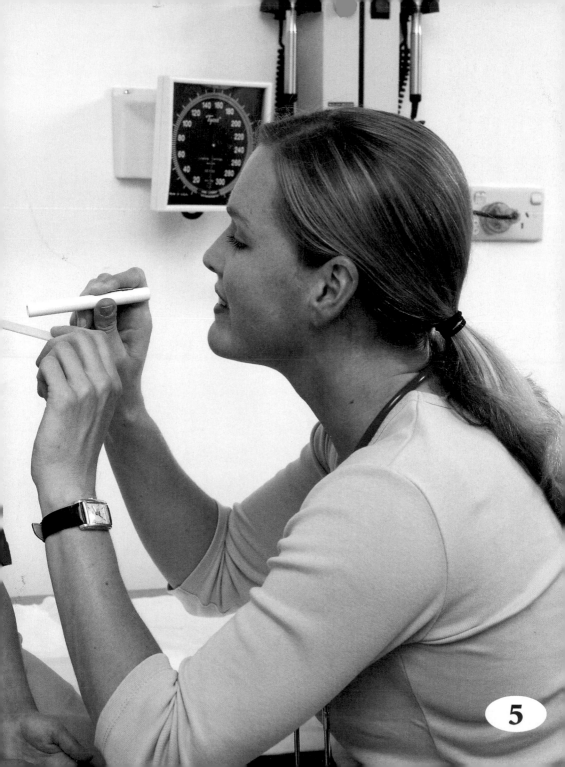

# My doctor takes care of me.

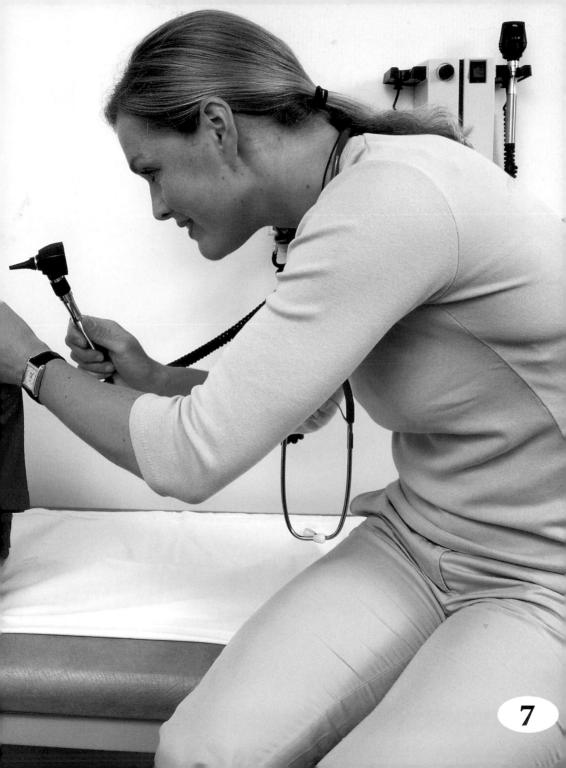

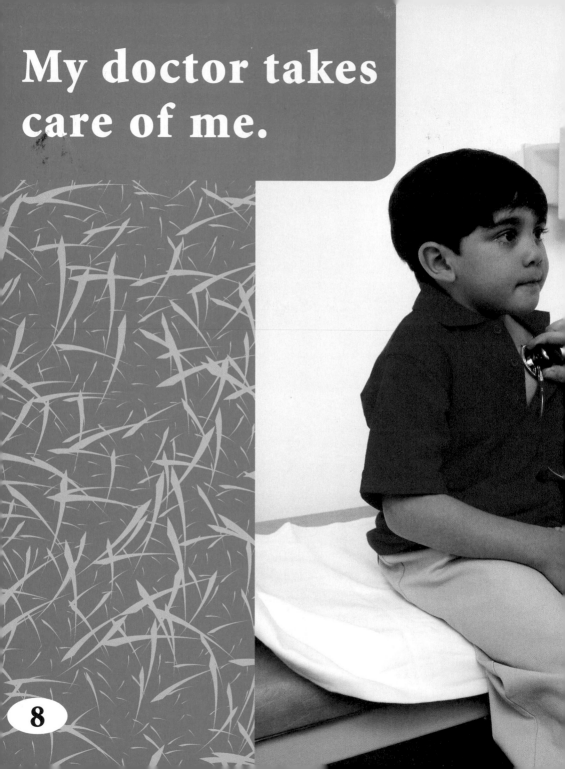

# My doctor takes care of me.

# My doctor takes care of me.

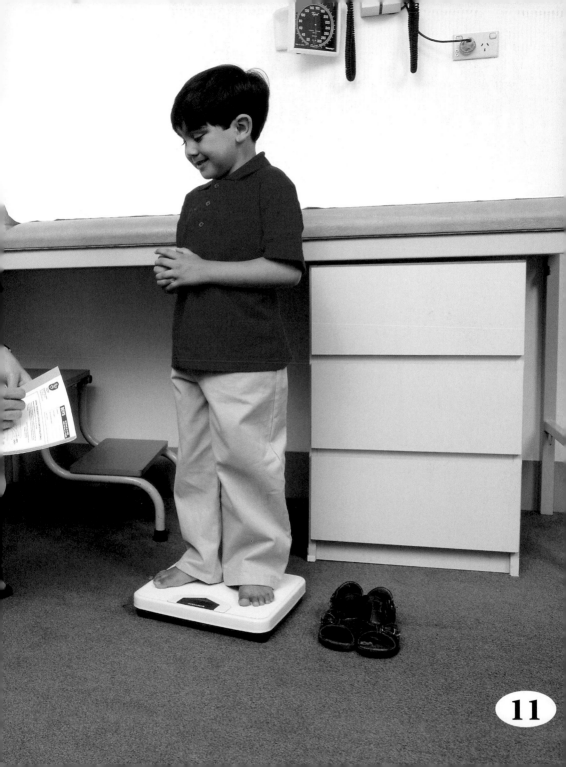

11

# My doctor takes care of me.

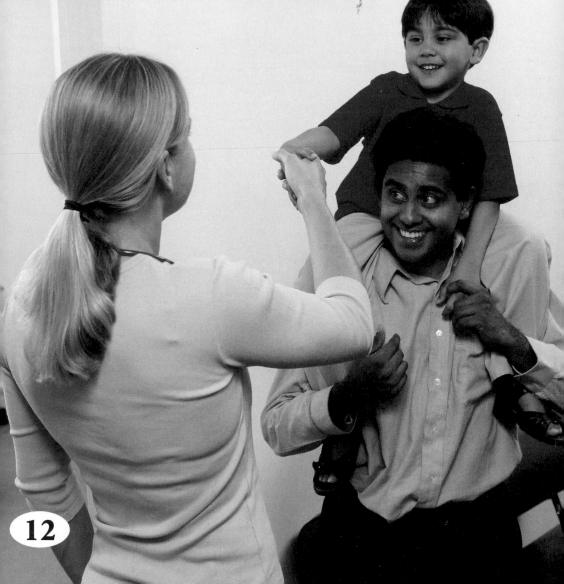